Zürich Travel Highlights

Best Attractions & Experiences

Jon Braithwaite

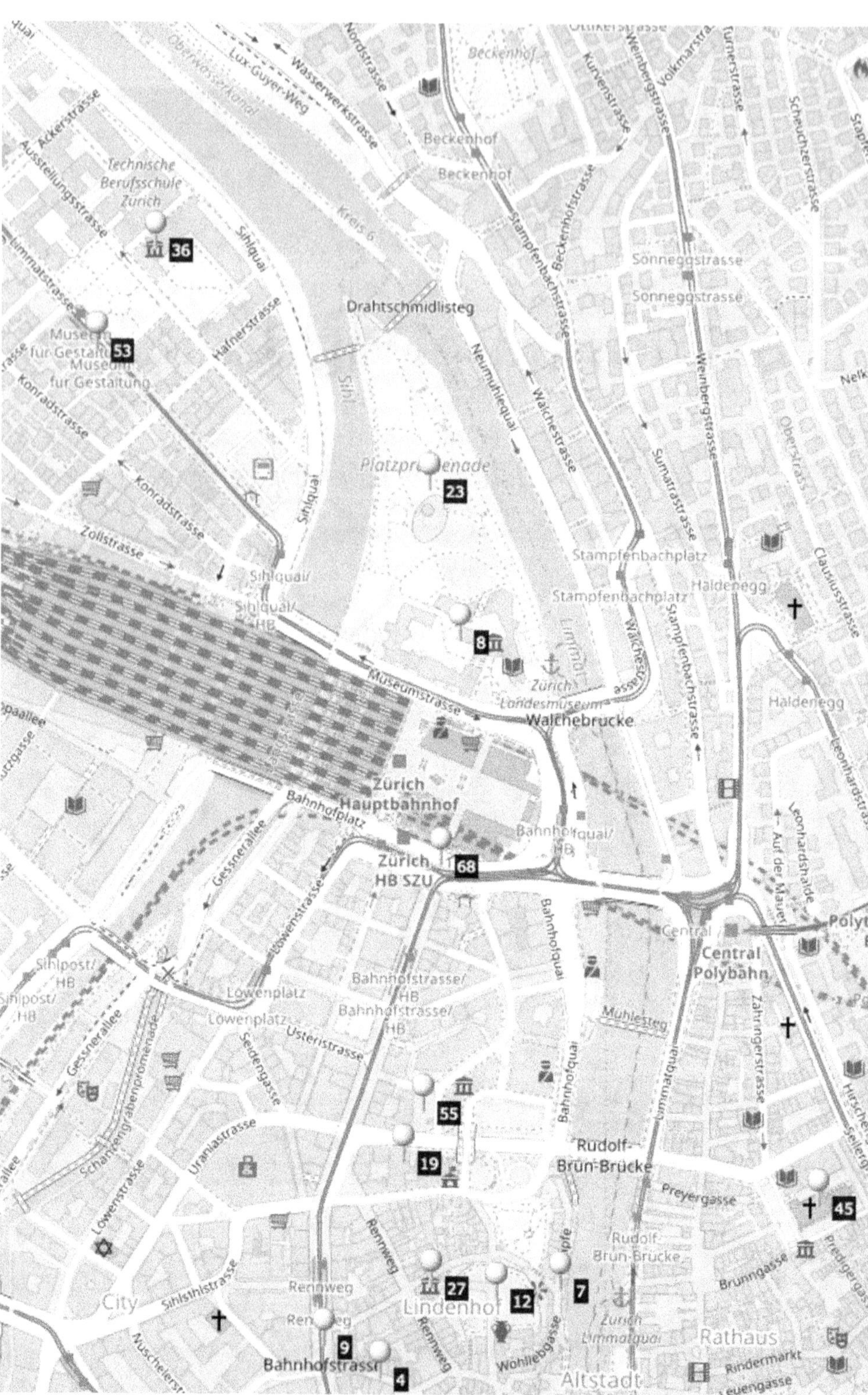

Beckenhof
Ottikerstrasse
Weinbergstrasse
Volkmarstrasse
Turnerstrasse
Scheuchzerstrasse
Stapferstrasse
Nordstrasse
Kurvenstrasse
Wasserwerkstrasse
Oberwieser-Kanal
Lux-Guyer-Weg
Beckenhof
Beckenhof
Sönneggstrasse
Sönneggstrasse
Ackerstrasse
Ausstellungsstrasse
Technische
Berufsschule
Zürich
Kreis 6
Stampfenbachstrasse
Beckenhofstrasse
Sihlquai
36
Limmatstrasse
Museum
für Gestaltung
Museum
für Gestaltung
Hafnerstrasse
Drahtschmidlisteg
Neumühlequai
Walchestrasse
Sumatrastrasse
Weinbergstrasse
Oberstrasse
Nelken
Konradstrasse
53
Sihl
Platzpromenade
23
Stampfenbachplatz
Konradstrasse
Zollstrasse
Sihlquai/
Sihlquai/
HB
Museumstrasse
Stampfenbachplatz
Stampfenbachstrasse
Haldenegg
Walchestrasse
Clausiusstrasse
8
Zürich
Landesmuseum
Walchebrücke
Haldenegg
spaallee
zgasse
Zürich
Hauptbahnhof
Bahnhofplatz
Gessnerallee
Zürich
HB SZU
Bahnhofquai/
HB
68
Bahnhofquai
Leonhardstrasse
Leonhardshalde
Auf der Mauer
Central
Polyter
ET
Sihlpost/
HB
Sihlpost/
HB
Gessnerallee
Löwenplatz
Löwenplatz
Usteristrasse
Bahnhofstrasse/
HB
Bahnhofstrasse/
HB
Central
Polybahn
Mühlesteg
Zähringerstrasse
Schanzengrabenpromenade
Uraniastrasse
Seidengasse
Bahnhofquai
Rudolf-
Brün-Brücke
Hirschengraben
Seilergraben
Löwenstrasse
Schanzenstrasse
Sihlstrasse
City
55
19
Rennweg
Rennweg
Rennweg
Preyergasse
45
Brunngasse
Lindenhof
27
12
7
Rudolf
Brün-Brücke
Zürich
Limmatquai
Rathaus
9
Bahnhofstrasse
4
Wohllebgasse
Altstadt
Rindermarkt
Neuengasse

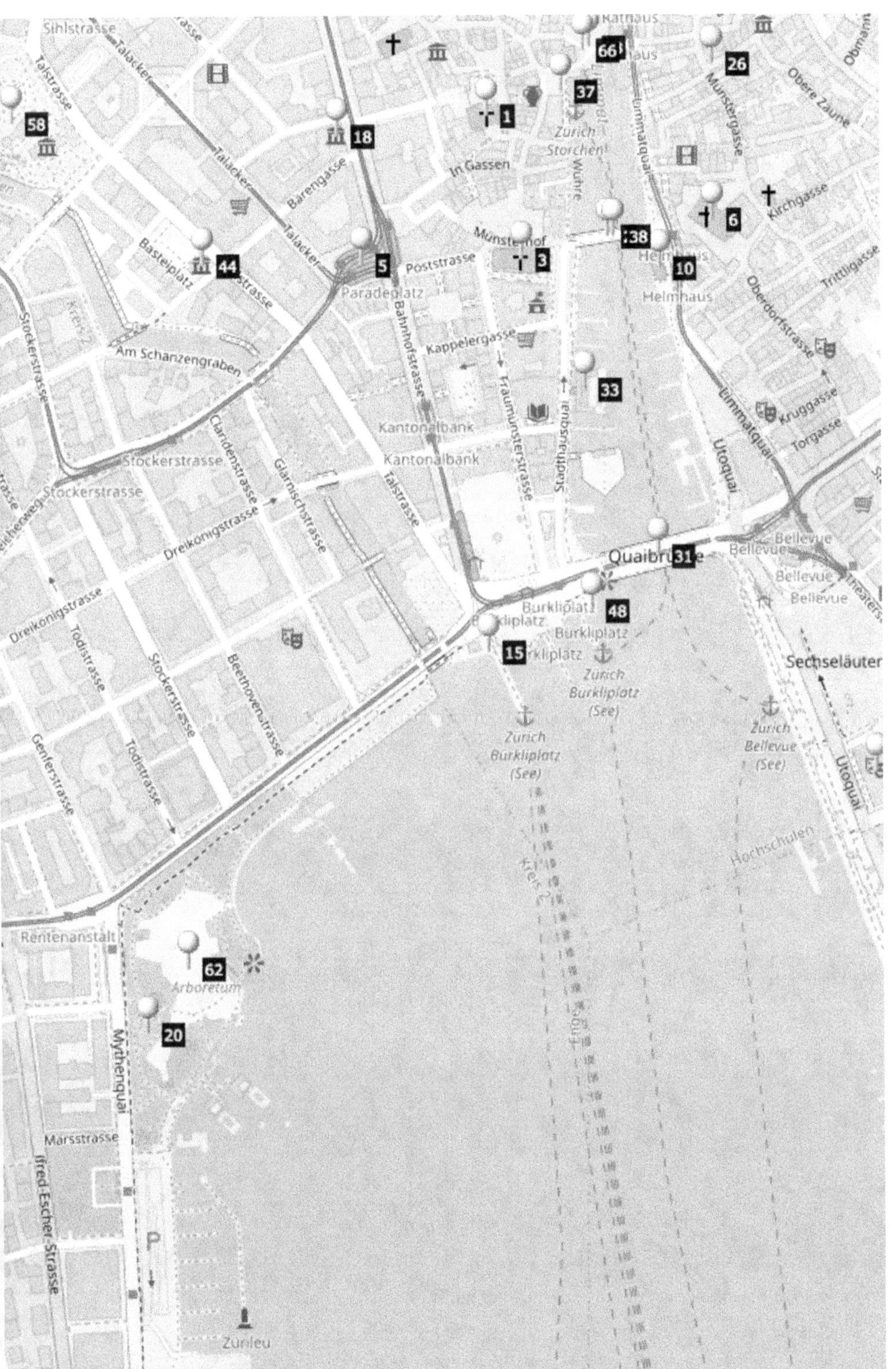

Sihlstrasse
Talacker
Talstrasse
58
18
Barengasse
Bärengasse
In Gassen
Zürich Storchen
Münsterhof
Münstergasse
Obere Zäune
Obmann
26
66
37
1
Kirchgasse
6
Zürich Wühre
38
Helmhaus
10
Helmhaus
Oberdorfstrasse
Trittligasse
Basteiplatz
44
5
Poststrasse
Paradeplatz
Bahnhofstrasse
Kappelergasse
3
33
Fraumünsterstrasse
Stadthausquai
Limmatquai
Utoquai
Kruggasse
Torgasse
Am Schanzengraben
Claridenstrasse
Stockerstrasse
Stockerstrasse
Kantonalbank
Kantonalbank
Glarnischstrasse
Talstrasse
Dreikonigstrasse
Dreikönigstrasse
Stockerstrasse
Beethovenstrasse
Todistrasse
Tödistrasse
Genferstrasse
Bellevue
Bellevue
Bellevue
Bellevue
Bellevue Theaters.
Quaibrü... 31
Sechseläuten
Bürkliplatz
48
Bürkliplatz
15
Bürkliplatz
Zürich Bürkliplatz (See)
Zürich Bürkliplatz (See)
Zürich Bellevue (See)
Utoquai
Kreis 2
Engel...
Hochschulen
Rentenanstalt
62
Arboretum
20
Mythenquai
Marsstrasse
Alfred-Escher-Strasse
P
Zürleu

Contents

Welcome to Zürich

The city of Zürich is a global center for commerce and finance. Its Old Town is on the banks of the Limmat River, and features picturesque medieval bridges connecting picturesque cobblestone streets with stone buildings. The area also has two of the most famous churches in Switzerland, Fraumünster church and Grossmünster church.

☐ 1. St. Peter's Church

Address: St. Peterhofstatt, 8001 Zürich, Switzerland

Phone: +41 044 221 06 74

Email: lilo.daetwyler@zh.ref.ch

Web: http://st-peter-zh.ch/

Built in 1489, St. Peter's Church is the largest clock tower in Europe, with a diameter of almost 9 meters. Do not miss the chance to look inside the church as well, since the interior is beautifully decorated by paintings and frescoes that will draw your attention. The outside of the church is equally attractive, with its 70-meter-high spire giving it an air of nobility. The clock itself was made by master clockmaker Atila Ilgaz, who created another masterpiece at Piazza San Marco's bell tower in Venice.

☐ 2. Old Town Zurich

Address: 1 Wühre, Zürich 8001, Switzerland

Walk through history with a stroll through Zurich's Old Town. It is considered to be one of the best preserved medieval city centers in Europe, and it is where your adventure begins. Plan on browsing the many shops along the way and enjoying a meal in one of the many restaurants or cafes. You can also visit one of the local bars where you will most likely hear live music and feel the rhythm of Zurich. This area has everything for your enjoyment, and we know you'll enjoy it as much as we do.

□ 3. Fraumünster Church

Address: Münsterhof 2, 8001 Zürich, Switzerland
Phone: +41 44 22 12 063
Email: info@fraumuenster.ch

The Fraumünster Church boasts an impressive set of stained glass windows created by Marc Chagall between 1978 and 1984. Of the 750 square meters of colored glass, 240 depict

New Testament scenes, while the remaining panels represent traditional religious symbolism enriched with secular images inspired by the French Renaissance. Built in 853 on the site of a former abbey for aristocratic women, today this place is open to believers and curious visitors alike.

☐ 4. Augustiner Street

Address: 34 Augustinergasse, Zürich 8001, Switzerland

The streets and squares of this area, right in the heart of the Zürich city centre, are so steep that you can imagine yourself being in ancient Rome when strolling here. The Augustiner Street is located in the city's medieval-old town, which dates back to 853. The entire street is lined with colourful houses, which have been reconstructed to look exactly like they did in the Middle Ages. It is a great place to just aimlessly stroll about, wander through the many small shops and stalls offering a wide variety of trinkets and goods, and just enjoy the atmosphere.

☐ 5. Parade Square

Address: 11 Paradeplatz, Zürich 8001, Switzerland

Paradeplatz is the name of a central square in Zürich. It is one of Zürich's most famous and popular places not only with locals but also with tourists. The main reason for this is location: it has outstanding connectivity, being located on the Plateau at the very heart of the city and served by 3 underground (Uetliberg and

Hardbrücke stations, and Bellevue station), 4 tram (line 2 and 8) and bus (lines 10, 12, 14, 15 and 20) routes.

☐ 6. Grossmünster Church

Address: Grossmünsterplatz, 8001 Zurich, Switzerland
Phone: +41 44 250 66 50
Email: sekretariat.grossmuenster@zh.ref.ch
Web: https://www.grossmuenster.ch/

The Grossmünster Church is one of the main landmarks in the oldest part of Zürich. It's steep-roofed basilica dating back to the 10th century, provides the unmistakable backdrop to the city's Limmat Valley. The Grossmuenster has been destroyed by fire three times over the centuries, but since 1415 it has undergone no structural changes. It has been the setting for many coronations, weddings and other political events over the centuries.

☐ 7. Schipfe District

Address: Schipfe, 8001 Zurich, Switzerland

The Schipfe District of Zürich is located on the eastern slope of the Lindenhof, by the river Limmat. A residential district in the centre of the city, it's known for its Bellevueplatz square, which offers views overlooking Lake Zurich, and has some of Zürich's most stunning historical sites. It's also home to some of Zürich's most renowned restaurants, cafés, art galleries and boutiques. The Schipfe Church was built in 1392, and parts of it are protected as cultural property.

☐ 8. Swiss National Museum

Address: Museumstrasse 2, 8001 Zurich, Switzerland
Phone: +41 44 218 65 11
Email: info@snm.admin.ch
Web: https://www.nationalmuseum.ch/

The Swiss National Museum is located in the city of Zurich, and is the largest and most comprehensive of its kind in Switzerland. Its exhibits feature around 200,000 pieces from Switzerland's prehistory to the modern day—including tools, equipment, furniture, and much more. The museum building itself dates back to 1898 and was built in the Renaissance Revival style by Gustav Gull.

☐ 9. Bahnhof Street

Address: Bahnhofstrasse, 8001 Zurich, Switzerland
Phone: +41 43 243 90 00
Email: info@bahnhofstrasse-zuerich.ch

The Bahnhofstrasse is the historical hub of Zürich. It stretches from the Fraumünster church in the west to the city hall in the east, over a distance of approximately one kilometre. The construction of the streetscape in 1865 marked an important step in the development of the city centre, with streets being laid out across what had previously been moats resulting from the fortifications of Altstetten and Enge when Zürich became a member of the Swiss Confederation in 1351. This area was home to some of Zürich's most prominent citizens in the 15th century.

☐ 10. Water Church

Address: Limmatquai 31, 8001 Zurich, Switzerland
Phone: +41 44 251 61 77

The Wasserkirche of Zurich is a historic site located on a small island between the Limmat and the Aare rivers, in the old town of Zürich. The former abbey church was constructed from 1340 to 1439, and is built over a vaulted tunnel that was part of the river rerouting measures of 1442. It was one of the seven churches or chapels that were built in this region alongside the city walls. Today it is still in use as an active church including services in summer months.

☐ 11. Opera House

Address: Falkenstrasse 1, 8008 Zurich, Switzerland

Phone: +41 44 268 66 66

Email: tickets@opernhaus.ch

Web: https://www.opernhaus.ch/

The Zürich Opera House is the symbol of Zürich. It has been the home of the opera and ballet companies since 1891. The world famous architect, Fellner & Helmer, designed the building to be an integral part of the city's lakefront. With its impressive combination of elegant lines, large spaces, natural lighting and modern technical equipment, it presents a unique experience for artists, visitors and townspeople alike.

☐ 12. Lindenhof Hill

Address: 3 Pfalzgasse, Zürich 8001, Switzerland

The Lindenhof is a hill in the historical center of the city of Zürich. It is one of the central and most popular sites in the old town of Zürich. The area, which includes remains from prehistoric times to the late middle ages, is listed in the Swiss inventory of cultural property of national and regional significance as a "Class A" site.

☐ 13. Chinese Garden

Address: Bellerivestrasse 138, 8008 Zürich
Phone: +41 44 380 31 51

The Chinese Garden is a gift from the city of Kunming, the capital of Yunnan Province in Southwest China. It was dedicated to the people of Zürich on behalf of the three official friends of winter: pine, bamboo and plum tree. The Chinese Garden is a unique synthesis of East and West. Like its sister garden, the Japanese Garden, it entices visitors into a relaxed mood and anchors them in space and time.

☐ 14. Lakeside Promenade

Address: Mythenquai 301, 8038 Zürich, Switzerland

The promenade is a lakeside walkway located in Zürich. The promenade runs along the eastern shore and passes a number of statues and monuments, including the Lion Monument (lion monument) by Otto Schmidt-Hofer, created for the Federal Council of German-speaking Switzerland. It was inaugurated on August 6, 1939 for the hundredth anniversary of Swiss independence. A popular place for outdoor activities including walking, jogging or biking, it also hosts several annual events like the open air theatre festival Zürifäscht (Zurich Festival), which takes place in June.

☐ 15. Lake Cruises

Address: Mythenquai 333, 8038 Zürich, Switzerland
Phone: +41 44 487 13 33
Email: ahoi@zsg.ch
Web: http://www.zsg.ch/

Take a cruise in Zurich to discover the most beautiful sights of the city from the Lake. You can choose between two-, three- or four-hour cruises, all of which offer stunning views over the lake, night cruises with lighted buildings, sightseeing cruises with commentary, romantic cruises with musical soundtracks, themed cruises with party accessories on board, and an exciting pirate adventure sail.

☐ 16. FIFA World Football Museum

Phone: +41 43 388 25 00
Email: info@fifamuseum.org
Web: http://www.fifamuseum.com/

Tour the FIFA World Football Museum in Zurich, an interactive museum that brings to life the history of football - be it through exhibitions or fascinating interactive cabinets. The museum aims at educating visitors of all ages about the history of their favourite game, citing hundreds of artefacts and history-rich objects on display in more than 4,000 square meters of space.

☐ 17. Kunsthaus Zürich

Address: Heimplatz 1, 8001 Zurich, Switzerland
Phone: +41 44 253 84 84
Email: info@kunsthaus.ch
Web: http://www.kunsthaus.ch/

The Kunsthaus Zürich is the most important exhibition space for contemporary art in Switzerland. The present building, designed by architect Mario Botta, was erected in 1995 and opened in June 1996. It is an example of avant-garde architecture and a premiere venue for international artists. Maintained by the local art association called Zürcher Kunstgesellschaft, this museum is dedicated to collecting and exhibiting works of art that depict the culture and history of Zürich and its surroundings.

□ 18. Clock and Watch Museum Beyer

Address: Bahnhofstrasse 31, 8001 Zürich, Switzerland

Phone: +41 043 344 63 63

Web: https://www.beyer-ch.com/de/uhrenmuseum/

The Beyer Museum is one of the world's most important clock and watchmaking museums. Established in 1939, it is housed in a listed historical building situated at the corner of Bahnhofstrasse and Rämistrasse, the main shopping boulevards of Zürich's old town. The ground floor was acquired by Friedrich Beyer in 1864. With its rich collections, the Uhrenmuseum Beyer preserves both watches belonging to renowned pioneers of watchmaking and outstanding masterpieces from later periods, ranging from the early 16 th century up to the latest creations.

☐ 19. Urania Observatory

Address: Uraniastrasse 9, 8001 Zurich, Switzerland
Phone: +41 43 317 16 40
Email: sarah.mueller@urania-sternwarte.ch
Web: http://www.urania-sternwarte.ch/

Urania Sternwarte is a public observatory in the Lindenhof quarter of Zürich. The 65 cm-diameter Zeiss double refractor built by Carl Zeiss (Jena) was mounted on 25 April 1904. It was modernized and moved to its present location in the 1950s.

Since 1 July 2010 Urania is operated by an association that has as partners University of Zürich and ETH Zürich as well as the City of Zurich and the Astronomical Society of Zürich.

☐ 20. Aviary Zurich

Address: Mythenquai 1, 8002 Zurich, Switzerland
Phone: +41 1 201 05 36
Email: info@voliere.ch
Web: http://www.voliere.ch/

Take your kids to Aviary Zürich for interactive fun that will be enjoyed by both you and your children. Get up close to more than 40 exotic bird species, including parrots, toucans, pelicans, flamingos, vultures, cormorants, egrets and many others. This bird sanctuary boasts a lush green lawn with plenty of places to sit and enjoy a picnic depending on the season.

☐ 21. Succulent Collection

Address: Mythenquai 1, 8002 Zurich, Switzerland
Phone: +41 043 344 34 80
Web: https://www.stadt-zuerich.ch/sukkulenten

Succulent plants live in arid or dry environments with little water, yet have developed a number of adaptations to deal with this problem. These adaptations typically include the formation of drought-resistant roots, stems and leaves. Sukkulenten-Sammlung Zürich is a private collection started by Alex Herzog in 1967. In 1991 this was made into a foundation funded by Zürich - Zentrum company, "Stiftung für die

Sukkulenten-Sammlung Zürich" which is now public and is subsidised by the City of Zürich since 1995.

□ 22. Botanical Garden

Address: Zollikerstrasse 107, University of Zurich, 8008 Zurich, Switzerland
Phone: +41 044 634 84 61
Email: botanischer.garten@systbot.uzh.ch
Web: http://www.bg.uzh.ch/

The Botanical Garden of the University of Zurich is located on Zollikerstrasse in the Weinegg quarter, outside the city center. Established in 1977, the garden now covers an area of 15 hectares and contains over 8000 different plant species. It makes use of various microclimates to cultivate plants native to various parts of the world. The humid greenhouse houses particularly humid-loving plants such as tree ferns, cacti, indoor palm trees, African violets and many others.

☐ 23. Platzpromenade

Address: Platzpromenade, Zürich 8006, Switzerland

In the vibrant city of Zürich, Platzpromenade stretches from one of Switzerland's main landmarks – Fraumünster Church –

to a major art and culture hub: the Kunsthaus. Along this 350m walkway, you will find everything from fresh produce to an impressive variety of shops and boutiques.

☐ 24. Zürihorn Park

Address: Bellerivestrasse 160, 8008 Zurich, Switzerland

A park located at the eastern end of Lake Zürich. It is named after the artificial Zürichhorn cape and protected as part of the Seefen and Füllungen nature reserve (within the Seefeld quarter). The park was created to protect and showcase the natural lake shore and to provide a recreational area for both residents and tourists.

☐ 25. Rietberg Museum

Address: Gablerstrasse 15, 8002 Zurich, Switzerland
Phone: +41 44 415 31 31
Email: museum.rietberg@zuerich.ch
Web: http://www.rietberg.ch/

The Rietberg Museum is a unique institution. It has been described as a city museum, a showcase for non-European art and design from all around the world - from the ancient world to the present day. Opened in 1898, it was one of the first museums in Switzerland dedicated to non-European art and design. Since 1931, the Rietberg Collection has been owned by the city of Zürich, together with four other major collections located in Zürich: the Swiss Museum of Transport, the Ethnological Museum, the Schweizerisches Landesmuseum and the Textile Museum.

☐ 26. Cabaret Voltaire

Address: Spiegelgasse 1, 8001 Zurich, Switzerland

Phone: +41 043 268 57 20

Email: duda@cabaretvoltaire.ch

Web: http://www.cabaretvoltaire.ch/

Cabaret Voltaire, Zürich. A café that was the site of many artfully surreal events and productions. Cabaret Voltaire was founded by Hugo Ball, with his companion Emmy Hennings, in the back room of Holländische Meierei, Spiegelgasse 1, on February 5, 1916 as a cabaret for artistic and political purposes. Other founding members were Marcel Janco, Richard Huelsenbeck, Tristan Tzara and Sophie Taeuber-Arp and Jean Arp.

☐ 27. Zurich Toy Museum

Address: Fortunagasse 15, 8001 Zurich, Switzerland
Phone: +41 044 211 93 05
Email: info@zuercher-spielzeugmuseum.ch
Web: http://www.zuercher-spielzeugmuseum.ch/

The Toy Museum is the only one of its kind in Europe. Since 1906, it has been displaying and preserving antique toys from all over Europe.

☐ 28. Rathausbrücke, Zürich

Address: 1 Rathausbrücke, Zürich 8001, Switzerland

A pedestrian bridge in the Swiss city of Zürich. The Rathausbrücke is the last bridge to cross the Limmat river before it joins with the Aare river. Also known as Gmüesbrugg, after the name of the former village at the Limmat crossing point, this popular public square connects Limmatquai with Weinplatz plaza and Schipfe quarter.

☐ 29. Museum of the History of Medicine

Address: Rämistrasse 69, University of Zurich, 8001 Zurich, Switzerland
Phone: +41 44 635 01 11
Email: info@iem.uzh.ch

The Museum of the History of Medicine, Zürich houses intriguing exhibits from the history of medicine from ancient times to the present day. From rare manuscripts to modern scientific instruments, as well as cured body parts and anatomical models this place has it all. The museum is housed in the former offices of Albert Einstein with an exciting and maybe a little scary exhibition on how medical science evolved.

☐ 30. Polyterasse

Address: 36 Leonhardstrasse, Zürich 8001, Switzerland

The Polyterasse, Zürich is a multi-purpose paved terrace lying on the roof of the Hochschulen (universities) Zürich. The surface area of 10,000 square meters makes it one of the largest and most impressive terraces of downtown Zurich.

☐ 31. Quaibrücke

Address: Quaibrücke, Zürich 8001, Switzerland

A Swiss icon, the Quaibrücke is a roadway and tramway bridge over the river Limmat, at the outflow of Lake Zürich. It was built simultaneously with the construction of Zürich's new quays between 1881 and 1887. From its own axis to the lakeside road, the Zürichberg (mountain), it provides passengers and transport links with an impressive panoramic view of lake and city.

☐ 32. Zürichberg (Hill)

The Zürichberg (Zurich Hill) is a wooded hill overlooking Lake Zürich and located immediately to the east of the city, between the valleys of the Limmat and the Glatt rivers. The highest point is about 270 metres above the Limmat and it is part of a chain of hills, such as Käferberg, Adlisberg and Forch and Pfannenstiel, between the Greifensee/Glattal and Lake Zürich.

☐ 33. Frauenbad Stadthausquai

Phone: +41 44 211 95 92

Frauenbad Stadthausquai is the only public bath for women in central Zürich, part of the historical Seeuferanlage promenades, featuring four outdoor swimming facilities.   It is at the Stadthausquai by Bürkliplatz plaza, built for women and still used for this purpose.   Built between 1881 and 1887, the facilities are listed in the Swiss inventory of cultural property of national and regional significance as a Class A attraction.

☐ 34. Constructive Art House

Address: Selnaustrasse 25, 8001 Zurich, Switzerland

Phone: +41 44 217 70 80

Email: info@hauskonstruktiv.ch

Web: http://hauskonstruktiv.ch/

The 'House for Constructive and Concrete Art', Haus Konstruktiv in Zurich, is a foundation and meeting place for contemporary art and culture. It aims to be a place of residence and refuge for promising artists and art groups who work in this field, as well as being a forum for public debate on artistic developments.

☐ 35. Freitag Store

Address: Geroldstrasse 17, 8005 Zurich, Switzerland

Phone: +41 43 366 95 20

Email: zurich@freitag.ch

The Freitag Store is a popular retail destination for a wide range of colourful bags and accessories from the Swiss Freitag label. Housed in an extraordinary building, the store offers both shoppers and visitors alike a unique shopping experience.

☐ 36. Museum of Design

Address: Ausstellungsstrasse 60, 8005 Zurich, Switzerland

Phone: +41 43 446 67 67

Email: welcome@museum-gestaltung.ch

Web: https://www.museum-gestaltung.ch/

The Museum of Design, Zürich presents the work of designers who have impacted the worlds of industry, culture, and business. Displaying more than 1000 pieces of furniture, photography, installations, product design, typography, graphic design, architecture, software design, web design, and art since 1956. The museum houses comprehensive archives for its exhibitions.

☐ 37. Winzerbrunnen Fountain

Address: 2 Weinplatz, Zürich 8001, Switzerland

The Winzerbrunnen is one of the most renowned fountains in Switzerland. It is located at the Lindenhof hill amid the Greifengasse and Rosengasse, Old Town, Zürich. This breathtaking fountain displays a clash of two different worlds – the medieval clash between science and faith and Renaissance period which emphasizes art and freedom of expression. The rich patina-green bronze bowls mimic a fountain, yet there appears to be a crater developing in the middle bowl because a clock is built into its center.

☐ 38. Münsterbrücke

Address: 1 Wühre, Zürich 8001, Switzerland

The Münsterbrücke, Zürich is a pedestrian and road bridge over the Limmat in the city of Zürich. It is listed in the Swiss inventory of cultural property of national and regional significance. It is named after the Fraumünster and Grossmünster.

☐ 39. Belvoirpark

Address: 137 Seestrasse, Zürich 8002, Switzerland

Belvoirpark is a vibrant quarter that attracts all kinds of people. To the east, the Zürichberg with its vineyards and ski-runs. To the west, the lake shore with one of the largest sailing centers in Switzerland. In between, there is a generous selection of shops and restaurants as well as a huge range of cultural events.

☐ 40. Rote Fabrik Music Venue

Address: Seestrasse 395, 8038 Zurich, Switzerland

Phone: +41 044 485 58 58

Email: info@rotefabrik.ch

Web: http://www.rotefabrik.ch/

Weaving together the creative talents of the world's greatest electronic music producers, Rote Fabrik has become one of the most respected live music venues in Zurich, Switzerland. First opened in 1996, this former textile factory in Zurich-Wollishofen has been attracting top international artists ever since. These include the likes of Richie Hawtin, Ricardo Villalobos, Luciano, DJ Hell, Sven Väth, Dave Clarke, and Jeff Mills.

☐ 41. Im Viadukt

Address: Viaduktstrasse 10, 8005 Zurich, Switzerland
Email: daniel.bollhalder@pwg.ch
Web: http://markthalle.im-viadukt.ch/

Im Viadukt offers a variety of designer shops, cafes and cultural venues. On the ground level you will find a supermarket, a kitchen shop, a salon and a cultural center with cinema, café and terrace. On the upper level there are restaurants with great views of the lake and city.

☐ 42. Moulagenmuseum

Address: 14 Haldenbachstrasse, Zürich 8006, Switzerland
Web: https://www.moulagen.uzh.ch/

Moulagenmuseum, Zürich showcases the lives of the ancient people from the Hallstatt period. It has been featured by National Geographic Television and other broadcasters, and it is regarded as one of the best places to experience how prehistoric man lived.

☐ 43. Zoo Zürich

Address: 36 Klosterweg, Zürich 8044, Switzerland
Web: https://www.zoo.ch/

The zoo's popular "Penguin Parade" takes place throughout the year. It is held hourly between 11 a.m. and 3 p.m., with the first showing at 11 a.m. The performance begins with the ringing of the Zoor bell, after which the keepers open the penguins' cages, and the birds waddle about an enclosed walkway for half an hour, led by a "penguinator" dressed in a tuxedo.

☐ 44. Gasthaus zum Bären

Web: http://www.gasthauszumbaeren.ch/

The Bären, with its striking wrought-iron staircase, Art Nouveau stained glass windows, and traditional wooden panelling, was one of the most popular restaurants and hotels in Switzerland in its day.   The Gasthaus zum Bären, Zürich is located in the historic Bahnhof district.   Located at the junction of the Limmatquai promenade and Lake Zurich peninsula this central location provides an excellent starting point to discover the city's attractions.   The famous street musicians of Zurich will play for you on the corner of Marktgasse and Bahnhofstrasse on any given evening.

□ 45. Predigerkirche

Web: http://www.predigerkirche.ch/

The Predigerkirche, Zürich is a church with a long history. The church was first started in about 1310 and was officially completed in 1483. Now it's a Lutheran church and is a popular tourist destination as well as a popular wedding venue.

□ 46. Coninx-Museum

Address: 32 Heuelstrasse, Zürich 8032, Switzerland

Over the past few years, innovative artistic projects have been realized in the Coninx-Museum, Zürich. The museum is associated with the Kunsthalle Zürich, where it has its own exhibition space in the heart of the city. Its focus is on new contemporary art in relation to traditional art forms.

□ 47. Migros Museum for Contemporary Art

Address: Limmatstrasse 270, 8005 Zurich, Switzerland
Phone: +41 44 272 15 15
Web: http://www.kunsthallezurich.ch/

The Migros Museum für Gegenwartskunst is a contemporary art museum in Zurich. The museum was founded in 1998. It houses an approximately 3,500 square meters large exhibition space on two floors for temporary exhibitions of contemporary art from around the world.

☐ 48. Bürkliplatz

Address: General-Guisan-Quai, Zürich 8001, Switzerland

The Bürkliplatz is a town square situated at the heart of Zürich. It is one of the busiest squares in Switzerland and a popular tourist destination. The square was first mentioned as a city market place in a document dated 994 AD.

☐ 49. Pavillon Le Corbusier

Web: https://www.pavillon-le-corbusier.ch/

Pavillon Le Corbusier, Zürich is an iconic landmark that consists of two concrete roofs that form a roof garden. The roof design features streamlined precursors to the contemporary free-form architectural style seen in today's curved roofs. The institution is used as office space for companies and individuals; an arts venue; and is open the general public. Each year, it receives around one million visitors.

☐ 50. Schauspielhaus

Address: Rämistrasse 34, 8001 Zurich, Switzerland
Phone: +41 044 258 7777
Web: http://www.schauspielhaus.ch/

The Schauspielhaus Zürich is one of the most prominent and important theatres in the German-speaking world. It is also known as Pfauenbühne – the Swan stage. The large theatre has 750 seats and is situated directly on Rennweg and close to the river Limmat. The Schauspielhaus also operates three stages in the Schiffbau in the western part of Zürich, the Schiffbau/Halle, Schiffbau/Box and Schiffbau/Matchbox.

☐ 51. Rote Fabrik

Address: 409 Seestrasse, Zürich 8038, Switzerland

The Rote Fabrik, Zürich is a creative space for social and political engagement in the city of Zürich. The name "Rote Fabrik" is a homonym to the name of an old textile factory that occupied the same site from the 1920s until 1981. In our time, the former factory premises house a variety of cultural and artistic organizations, each with its own concept and character - organizers of festivals, concerts, film screenings, debates and readings.

□ 52. Heureka Science Museum

Address: 160 Bellerivestrasse, Zürich 8008, Switzerland

Experience the Heureka, one of the city's most popular attractions for children and adults alike. This interactive science museum provides visitors with an entertaining and informative learning experience, with dozens of fun exhibits encompassing everything from technology to zoology.

□ 53. Plakatraum (Poster-Room)

Address: Limmatstrasse 55, 8005 Zurich, Switzerland
Phone: +41 43 446 44 66
Email: plakatsammlung@museum-gestaltung.ch

The Plakatraum (Poster-Room), the world's largest collection of posters, was founded in Zürich in 1947. The large shop of posters sells complete series (the "Weltposterserie" for example) as well as special collections and individual posters.

☐ 54. Stadelhoferplatz

Address: 16 Goethestrasse, Zürich 8001, Switzerland

Bordered by the Limmat River on one side and the Äussere Kanal on the other, Stadelhofen is a quiet but beautifully historic neighborhood located in the heart of the city. What makes Stadelhoferplatz unique is its vibrant mix of historic buildings, modern architecture, beautiful views of the cityscape, and charming parks scattered throughout.

☐ 55. Werdmühleplatz

Address: 6 Werdmühleplatz, Zürich 8001, Switzerland

The Werdmühleplatz, Zürich is a small square in the center of the old town of Zurich. The square belongs to the district Seegarten and is one of the smallest public squares in Europe. It is renowned for its imposing water jet fountain. The square takes its name from an old mill which used to be located here called respectively "Werd" or "Werrmühle". The word was probably also derived from the local dialect word "Werr" which means Wiese (meadow).

□ 56. Fluntern Cemetery

Address: Zürichbergstrasse 189, 8044 Zurich, Switzerland
Phone: +41 044 251 87 00

Founded in 1808, this cemetery is operated by the city of Zürich. It is also known as Friedhof Fluntern, and was the first public graveyard in Switzerland. The cemetery features more than 1,000 tombstones, set amongst green lawns and mature trees. The cemetery houses the remains of notable members of Swiss society, including writer Carl Spitteler, ethnographer Adolf Friedrich Stenzler, designer Hans Hilfiker, and artists Sophie Taeuber-Arp and Benno Becker.

☐ 57. Bernhard Theater

Phone: +41 44 268 66 99
Web: https://www.bernhardtheater.ch/

The Bernhard Theater, Zürich is a pubic theatre that was designed by the architects Peter Böhm and Norbert Aepli, and opened in 1991. The construction of the hall is a feat worth seeing. It is a building with a ravine underneath it which has been done on a scale worthy of a theatrical illusion. This ravine provides the theater with stone from which the building was constructed. The stones used include jade from Greenland, granite from Bern and marble from Arona.

☐ 58. Alter Botanischer Garten

Address: 40 Pelikanstrasse, Zürich 8001, Switzerland

Known to be among the oldest botanical gardens in the world, the Garden of Old Botany started its history back in 1593. In 1859, it was moved from its previous site outside of the city to where it now resides, next to the Hofwyl Castle and a short drive from Zürich Main Station. Dating back to 1642, Hofwyl Castle was once owned by a renowned family who played a big role in Swiss politics. Today, Hofwyl Castle is a five-stars hotel offering a wide range of facilities and services.

☐ 59. Rieterpark

Address: Zürich 8002, Switzerland

The Rieterpark is not only one of the largest inner city parks, but also one of the most popular. It is particularly known for its many trees, its large rose garden and the nearby Kunsthalle. The Rieterpark also houses an outdoor concert arena, which is regularly used for open-air events in summer. Just off the park, near Bellevueplatz, there stands a statue to Zwingli, a prominent Swiss cleric from the 16th century.

□ 60. Ruine Dübelstein

Address: 95 Schloss-Strasse, 8600, Switzerland

The Ruine Dübelsteighas served as a fortress and stronghold in the town of Zürich since 1273. The castle sits high on a hill overlooking the city and Lake Zurich, with the immediate neighborhood sporting many luxurious houses. It is an excellent example of late Romanesque secular architecture in Switzerland, with its massive walls and two towers. This castle is listed as a Swiss heritage site of national significance.

☐ 61. Thermalbath & Spa Zurich

Address: Brandschenkestrasse 150, 8002 Zurich, Switzerland
Phone: +41 044 205 96 50
Email: info@thermalbad-zuerich.ch
Web: http://www.thermalbad-zuerich.ch/

The Thermalbath & Spa is located in the bank vaults of the prestigious and charming Baur au Lac on Seefeldquai. The premises with thermal spa, rooftop pool and open air water tubs are located in the city center at the scenic Seeufer (waterfront) promenade of Lake Zurich. This idyllic location with one of Europe's most beautiful lakes in the background offers views of the glittering downtown skyscrapers and the glistening snow-capped Alps.

☐ 62. Arboretum

Address: Zürich 8002, Switzerland

The Arboretum, Zürich is a park set in the middle of Switzerland's largest city. This park consists of a botanical garden and outdoor zoological park. The botanical garden is divided into five sections: medicinal plants, conifer and broad-leaved trees, beech and maple trees, alpine plants and alpine garden, and aromatic plants and medicinal herbs. These sections cover over 13 hectares (32 acres). The garden holds 9800 different plant species including conifers like cedars, pines and deodars (coniferous evergreens from Himalayas).

☐ 63. Loorenkopf

The Loorenkopf is a lookout tower and an observation platform up to 33 meters high and is located on Adlisberg, north of Witikon in Zurich at 694 m above sea level. The octagonal tower made of rough-hewn wood was opened in September 1954. In the frame there are 153 steps to the top. From here you have a view of the Alps including the Eiger, Mönch and Jungfrau.

☐ 64. Tiefenbrunnen Beach

Address: Bellerivestrasse 200, 8008 Zurich, Switzerland

Phone: +41 44 422 32 00

Bethlehem Beach lies on the shore of Lake Zürich west of Wollishofen. It has a chute, a slippery slide and a playground for children as well as a beach bar. There are many restaurants and several boat moorings as well as a large number of boats with local fishermen. The Tiefenbrunnen lakeside is the largest lakeside within the city boundaries and has 21,000 square meters of lawn and trees, 2900 square meters of sand and 1300 square meters of grass and rocks.

□ 65. Theater Winkelwiese

Address: 4 Winkelwiese, Zürich 8001, Switzerland
Web: http://www.winkelwiese.ch/

Theater Winkelwiese is a theater located in Zürich. The theater presents musical performances as well as silent film projections and live shows. Theater Winkelwiese is known for its programs dedicated to the origins of cinema and the exploration of early film technology.

☐ 66. Rathausbrücke

Address: 10 Weinplatz, Zürich 8001, Switzerland

This bridge crosses the Limmat River and is 425 meters (1,394 ft) long. Since its completion in 1982, the Rathausbrücke has remained one of Switzerland's most emblematic bridges. The structure features three pylons with streetlamps shaped like obelisks on top of them.

☐ 67. Uhrenmuseum zum Rösli

Address: 46 Röslistrasse, Zürich 8006, Switzerland
Web: https://www.uhrenmuseumroesli.ch/

The Uhrenmuseum zum Rösli specializes in clocks, watches and timekeepers from 1530 to 1950 and is organized in various rooms: a museum room, a workshop and an office. It is one of the only private museums for clocks and watches in Switzerland. The Uhrenmuseum zum Rösli collects clocks and timekeepers from all over Europe. It concentrates on historical timekeepers such as mechanical pocket watches, domestic clocks and old tower clocks.

☐ 68. Alfred Escher-Statue

Address: 15 Bahnhofplatz, Zürich 8001, Switzerland

The Alfred Escher Statue is one of the Zürich's best known monuments. It shows Alfred Escher (1819–1882), an eminent Swiss politician, five times President of the Swiss National Council (the Parliament) and founder of the Schweizerische Kreditanstalt (Credit Suisse). His statue is located in front of the Swiss National Museum in downtown Zürich.

Picture Credits

Zürich, Switzerland Cover: Sonyuser / 4636745 (Pixabay)

St. Peter's Church: Roland Zh (CC BY-SA 3.0)

Old Town Zurich: Albinfo (PD)

Fraumünster Church: Andrew Bossi (CC BY-SA 2.5)

Augustiner Street: Roland Zh (CC BY-SA 3.0)

Parade Square: Andreas Praefcke (CC BY 3.0)

Grossmünster Church: Крізь Час (CC BY-SA 4.0)
Schipfe District: Roland Zh (CC BY-SA 3.0)
Swiss National Museum: Roland Zh (CC BY-SA 3.0)
Bahnhof Street: Sidonius (PD)
Water Church: Roland Zh (CC BY-SA 3.0)
Opera House: Kuhnmi (CC BY 2.0)
Lindenhof Hill: Andrew Bossi (CC BY-SA 2.5)
Chinese Garden: Zairon (CC BY-SA 3.0)
Lakeside Promenade: Chris J Wood (CC BY-SA 3.0)
Lake Cruises: Nikater (PD)
Kunsthaus Zürich: Sailko (CC BY-SA 3.0)
Clock and Watch Museum Beyer: Natalia Sverdlova (CC BY-SA 3.0)
Urania Observatory: Juerg.Hug (CC BY-SA 3.0)
Aviary Zurich: Roland Zh (CC BY-SA 3.0)
Succulent Collection: James Steakley (CC BY-SA 3.0)
Botanical Garden: Juerg.Hug (CC BY-SA 3.0)
Platzpromenade: Roland Zh (CC BY-SA 3.0)
Zürihorn Park: Roland Zh (CC BY-SA 3.0)
Rietberg Museum: Ikiwaner (CC-BY-SA-3.0)
Cabaret Voltaire: Idem (CC BY 4.0)
Zurich Toy Museum: Flominator (CC BY-SA 3.0)
Rathausbrücke, Zürich: Adrian Michael (PD)
Museum of the History of Medicine: Roland Zh (CC BY-SA 3.0)
Quaibrücke: Roland Zh (CC BY-SA 3.0)
Zürichberg (Hill): Roland Zh (CC BY-SA 3.0)
Frauenbad Stadthausquai: Juerg.Hug (CC BY-SA 3.0)
Constructive Art House: Roland Zh (CC BY-SA 3.0)
Freitag Store: Micha L. Rieser (CC BY-SA 4.0)
Museum of Design: Roland Zh (CC BY-SA 3.0)
Münsterbrücke: Andyindia (CC BY-SA 3.0)
Belvoirpark: Roland Zh (CC BY-SA 3.0)

Rote Fabrik Music Venue: Adrian Michael (CC BY-SA 3.0)

Moulagenmuseum: Roland Zh (CC BY-SA 3.0)

Zoo Zürich: Mcaviglia (CC BY-SA 3.0)

Gasthaus zum Bären: Myriam Thyes (CC BY-SA 3.0)

Coninx-Museum: Adrian Michael (CC BY-SA 1.0)

Migros Museum for Contemporary Art: Roland Zh (CC BY-SA 3.0)

Schauspielhaus: Adrian Michael (CC BY 2.5)

Plakatraum (Poster-Room): Anonymous (PD)

Fluntern Cemetery: Albinfo (PD)

Alter Botanischer Garten: Roland Zh (CC BY-SA 3.0)

Rieterpark: Roland Zh (CC BY-SA 3.0)

Ruine Dübelstein: Adrian Michael (CC BY-SA 3.0)

Loorenkopf: Tschubby (CC-BY-SA-3.0)

Theater Winkelwiese: Roland Zh (CC BY-SA 3.0)

Alfred Escher-Statue: Anonymous (PD)

www.ingramcontent.com/pod-product-compliance
Lightning Source LLC
Chambersburg PA
CBHW061715130726
47996CB00006B/2317